BUDDY: AMERICA'S FIRST GUIDE DOG

by Meish Goldish

Consultants:
Michelle Barlak
Senior Associate, Public Relations
The Seeing Eye, Inc.

R. Bruce Johnson
Archivist
The Seeing Eye, Inc.
Morristown, New Jersey

New York, New York

Credits

Cover and Title Page, Courtesy The Seeing Eye; Contents, Courtesy The Seeing Eye; 4, Courtesy The Seeing Eye; 5, © Associated Press; 6, © John Keane; 7, © Starletdarlene/Dreamstime; 8, © Monika Wisniewska/Dreamstime; 9, Courtesy The Seeing Eye; 10, Courtesy The Seeing Eye; 11, Courtesy The Seeing Eye; 12, Courtesy The Seeing Eye; 13, © Anke Van Wyk/Dreamstime; 14, Courtesy The Seeing Eye; 15, Courtesy The Seeing Eye; 16, © Directphotocollection/Alamy; 17, Courtesy The Seeing Eye; 18, Courtesy The Seeing Eye; 19, Courtesy The Seeing Eye; 20, © David Burrows/Shutterstock; 21, Courtesy The Seeing Eye; 22, Courtesy The Seeing Eye; 23, © Bill Clark/Roll Call Photos/Newscom; 24, Courtesy The Seeing Eye; 25, Courtesy The Seeing Eye; 26L, © Jean Michel Labat/Agefotostock; 26R, © BSIP SA/Alamy; 27, Courtesy The Seeing Eye; 28, © Jeroen van den Broek/Shutterstock; 29TL, © Irina oxilixo Danilova/Shutterstock; 29TR, © Eric Isselée/Shutterstock; 29B, © Eric Isselée/Shutterstock.

Publisher: Kenn Goin
Editor: Jessica Rudolph
Creative Director: Spencer Brinker
Design: Dawn Beard Creative
Photo Researcher: We Research Pictures, LLC

The Seeing Eye is a 501(c)3 non-profit that breeds, raises, and trains Seeing Eye® dogs to guide people who are blind. For more information visit SeeingEye.org

Library of Congress Cataloging-in-Publication Data

Names: Goldish, Meish.
Title: Buddy : America's first guide dog / by Meish Goldish.
Description: New York, New York : Bearport Publishing, 2016. | Series: Dog
  heroes | Includes bibliographical references and index.
Identifiers: LCCN 2015037724| ISBN 9781943553099 (library binding) | ISBN
  1943553092 (library binding)
Subjects: LCSH: Buddy (Dog)—Juvenile literature. | Guide dogs—United
  States—Biography—Juvenile literature. | German shepherd dog—United
  States—Biography—Juvenile literature. | Guide dogs—Training of—United
  States—Juvenile literature. | Guide dog schools—United States—Juvenile
  literature.
Classification: LCC HV1780 .G65 2016 | DDC 362.4/1830929—dc23
LC record available at http://lccn.loc.gov/2015037724

For more information, write to Bearport Publishing Company, Inc., 45 West 21st Street, Suite 3B, New York, New York 10010. Printed in the United States of America.

10 9 8 7 6 5 4 3 2 1

Table of Contents

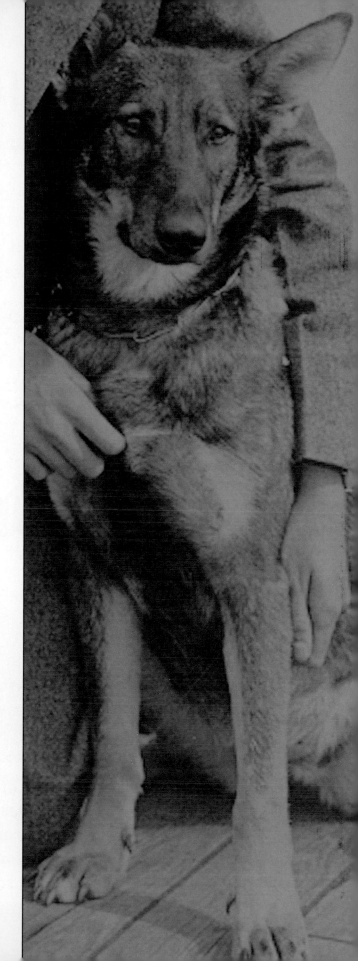

A Deadly Crossing

In June 1928, a German shepherd named Buddy stood at a corner on West Street in New York City. Cars and trucks zoomed by, but the dog stayed calm. Buddy was about to lead her blind owner, Morris Frank, across the busy road. Nobody in America had ever seen a dog guide a person who could not see.

Buddy guides Morris into West Street.

In 1928, most of New York City's streets, including West Street, had no traffic lights to tell drivers and **pedestrians** when to stop or go. Therefore, crossing streets was very dangerous and sometimes deadly.

A crowd of people, including newspaper reporters, gathered to watch the **historic** moment. Many people doubted the **canine** would succeed. West Street was the widest and busiest road in the city. It was so dangerous for pedestrians to cross that it was nicknamed "Death Street."

Stepping into the street with his dog, Morris started to worry. What if the noise and traffic were more than Buddy could handle? Would they reach the other side safely?

A busy street in New York City in the 1920s

Losing Sight

Before meeting Buddy, Morris had led a difficult life. He was born in Nashville, Tennessee, in 1908. At age six, Morris was blinded in one eye in a horse-riding accident. Ten years later, he lost sight in his other eye in a boxing match. Even though he could not see, Morris went to college. He also worked as a door-to-door salesman. However, human guides had to help him everywhere he went.

This human guide (right) is helping a person who is blind, similar to how Morris was helped by guides.

Morris didn't want to depend on other people to get around. His human guides were not reliable. Sometimes a guide would suddenly walk off the job, leaving Morris alone and in danger of falling or getting run over by a car. Morris wished he could be more **independent**.

PUSH BUTTON FOR PEDESTRIAN WARNING LIGHTS

←

CROSS WITH CAUTION

In the early 1900s, it was much harder for people who could not see to get around than it is today. There were no **guide dogs** or other forms of assistance, such as **braille** lettering on signs.

Braille letters and numbers are printed with raised dots that people can feel and read with their fingers.

Hopeful News

One day in 1927, Morris's father read him a magazine article written by Dorothy Eustis. Dorothy, an American living in Europe, trained German shepherds to work as **police dogs**. In her article, Dorothy described a school in Germany where dogs were trained to guide soldiers who had been blinded in war. She believed German shepherds should be trained to help more blind people in other parts of the world.

Today, police dogs are trained to use their noses to search for missing people or to sniff out illegal substances such as drugs.

German shepherds make good police dogs and guide dogs because they are strong and very intelligent.

Morris immediately sent a letter to Dorothy. He begged her to train a guide dog for him. In return, he offered to help her set up a school in America to teach other people how to use guide dogs. Morris wrote, "Train me and I will bring back my dog to show people here how a blind man can be absolutely on his own."

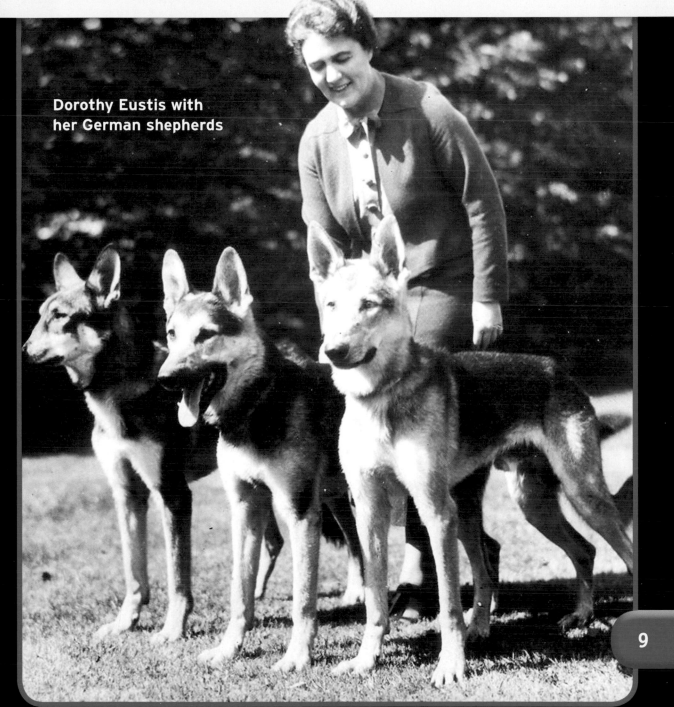

Dorothy Eustis with her German shepherds

Meeting a New Friend

After reading Morris's letter, Dorothy invited him to her **estate** in Switzerland, where she trained dogs. In April 1928, Morris sailed to Europe. At the estate, Morris was excited to meet his new dog, who was named Kiss. However, Morris decided to change her name to Buddy. He knew he would be embarrassed to say things in public, such as "Here, Kiss! Come, Kiss!"

Morris, Buddy, and Dorothy

On the ship to Europe, Morris wasn't allowed to walk around freely with the other passengers because he was blind. This made him angry and **determined** to help people who could not see gain more rights.

Buddy was gentle, sweet, and very smart—a perfect dog for Morris. An **instructor** named Jack Humphrey had already trained Buddy. Now he would train Morris, too. Jack taught him to attach a **harness** to Buddy and to hold it at all times, following the dog's lead as they walked. Buddy would move forward, left, or right based on Morris's **command**.

Morris training with Buddy

Keeping Morris Safe

Part of Buddy's training was learning how to keep Morris safe. Jack taught Buddy to stop and sit whenever she came to a street or steps. This signal told Morris to stop walking, feel around with his foot or a cane, and then step up or down.

During their training, Morris and Buddy grew very close.

Jack also taught Buddy when to **disobey** Morris. If Morris said, "Forward," but Buddy saw a gate or wall in front of them, she would refuse to step ahead. Morris sometimes missed Buddy's signals and stumbled down steps or bumped into gates. He had to work hard to pay close attention to the dog's movements.

One day during training, two horses got loose and ran toward Morris. As Morris gripped Buddy's harness, the dog ran up a hill out of the horses' path, saving her owner's life!

Success!

After five weeks of training, Morris returned to the United States with Buddy. News reporters met the pair in New York City. They wanted to see if the canine could guide Morris safely across West Street. Morris commanded, "Forward, Buddy," and the two stepped into the road.

Morris and Buddy crossing a city street

The heavy traffic was frightening. Several times, Buddy stopped and stepped back to avoid the oncoming cars and trucks. One truck sped by so close that Morris could feel the whoosh of air across his face. Yet Buddy stayed calm the entire time. When the two finally reached the other side, Morris gave his dog a big hug and said, "Good girl!"

Morris always hugged Buddy and praised her whenever she did a good job.

Morris described the dangerous crossing on West Street, "I shall never forget the next three minutes. Ten-ton trucks rocketing past, cabs blowing their horns in our ears, drivers shouting at us."

Back Home

Eventually, Morris returned with Buddy to his home in Tennessee. **Residents** were amazed by how well the guide dog helped Morris get around. In fact, Buddy helped not just Morris, but the townspeople as well. How?

Many people are interested to see a guide dog at work.

When Morris was blinded as a youth, many residents felt uncomfortable around him. They didn't know how to talk to him without bringing up his **disability**. However, with Buddy at his side, people found they could speak easily with Morris. Often they would start a conversation by saying, "What a lovely dog you have!" Buddy helped Morris make many new friends.

A harness on a dog identifies the canine as a working animal.

People should never pet a guide dog without the owner's permission. The dog is a working animal that shouldn't be **distracted** from its job.

The Seeing Eye

As the owner of America's first guide dog, Morris remembered the offer he had made to Dorothy. He planned to help her start a school in Nashville to teach students how to use guide dogs. Dorothy traveled to Tennessee to set up the school. Instructor Jack Humphrey also came to start the training program. In January 1929, the school, which was called The Seeing Eye, opened with just two students.

Jack Humphrey (left) stands with students and other instructors at The Seeing Eye school in 1929.

Over time, Nashville's **climate** proved to be too hot for the furry German shepherds. In 1931, The Seeing Eye was moved to New Jersey, where the school continued to grow. Soon, instructors there were training hundreds of students and dogs each year.

The Seeing Eye moved from Tennessee to New Jersey (above).

The first guide dogs used at The Seeing Eye were trained in Switzerland by Dorothy and Jack. Later, people in America **donated** their dogs to the school to be trained.

A Fight for Change

Morris was glad the school was doing well. However, he felt that more needed to be done to help people who couldn't see. In the 1930s, laws prevented guide dogs from entering public places such as stores and restaurants. Dogs also couldn't travel on planes, trains, or buses with their owners. Morris wanted to help give people who were blind the freedom to go anywhere.

NO DOGS ALLOWED

For many years, guide dogs were not allowed to enter public buildings.

Morris traveled with Buddy to many places to spread his message. He spoke to news reporters and lawmakers about letting guide dogs **accompany** their owners in public buildings and on public transportation. In time, his efforts paid off. By 1938, several railroads and one airline allowed guide dogs to ride with their owners.

Morris and Buddy step off a United Airlines plane after taking a trip in the late 1930s.

Morris traveled to the White House with Buddy twice. He spoke with Presidents Calvin Coolidge and Herbert Hoover about the need for new laws for guide dogs and their owners.

A New Buddy

Buddy was Morris's faithful **companion** for ten years, until she became ill and died in 1938. Morris had loved Buddy very much. It was difficult to get over her death. However, Morris knew he had to continue his work. He received another guide dog and named him Buddy II. Like the first Buddy, Morris's new dog served as a loyal guide and companion.

The first Buddy

Buddy was so famous that *The New York Times*, a major American newspaper, printed a story about the dog after her death.

Together, Morris and Buddy II traveled to many places, including **military** hospitals. Morris spoke to soldiers, doctors, and nurses about the importance of guide dogs. When Buddy II died in 1948, Morris buried him next to Buddy on the grounds of the **headquarters** of The Seeing Eye in New Jersey.

Soldiers blinded in battle can learn to live independent lives with guide dogs. This dog, named Gillian, (above) rests at the feet of her owner, Lieutenant Joseph Bozart, who lost his sight during an explosion in the Iraq War in 2006.

School Continues

Over the years, Morris had four more guide dogs, all of whom he named Buddy. Sadly, Morris Frank died in 1980. The school he helped create, The Seeing Eye, was now more than 50 years old. Thousands of its students had learned how to live independent lives with their canine companions.

A student from The Seeing Eye with her dog

Today, The Seeing Eye continues its important work. The school now **breeds** its own dogs. At eight weeks old, the puppies are given to **volunteers** who raise them and teach them basic commands. When the canines are a little over a year old, they return to The Seeing Eye for four months of training as guide dogs. Each dog is then paired with a blind student who becomes its owner. The pair train together for a month before leaving the school.

There are many guide dog schools in the United States and other countries. The Seeing Eye is the oldest guide dog school in the world.

The Seeing Eye breeds German shepherds, Labrador retrievers, golden retrievers, and Lab-golden mixes.

Buddies Still Needed

In recent times, guide dogs have become more helpful than ever. Years ago, traffic lights always changed after the same number of seconds, so people who were blind could **predict** when to cross the street. Today, however, many lights change according to the flow of traffic. People who are blind no longer know when a light will turn red or green. A guide dog can help them cross safely.

A guide dog leads a person across the street.

Some people who can't see use a guide dog, but many others use a long cane instead. The cane stretches about two steps ahead of the user and bumps against objects before the person can run into them.

It's also hard for a person to tell if a vehicle is coming just by listening. That's because today's cars are built to run more quietly. Guide dogs know to avoid cars—even those that make little or no noise. As Buddy first proved on West Street, a well-trained guide dog can be the eyes of freedom for those who cannot see.

A statue that honors Morris and Buddy is located in Morristown, New Jersey.

Just the Facts

- Since opening in 1929, The Seeing Eye has matched over 16,500 guide dogs with students. The average dog usually works about eight years. When a dog becomes too old to work, it can be kept as a pet or returned to The Seeing Eye and placed in a private home.

- In 1990, the U.S. Congress passed the Americans with Disabilities Act. This law says that people with disabilities cannot be kept out of offices, stores, trains, or other public places. Morris's and Buddy's hard work helped to make this law possible.

- Many people use the term *Seeing Eye dog* to mean *guide dog*. However, only dogs that are trained at The Seeing Eye can be called *Seeing Eye dogs*. For all canines trained at other dog-training schools for the blind, the correct term is *guide dog*.

Common Breeds:

GUIDE DOGS

golden retriever

Labrador retriever

German shepherd

accompany (uh-KUM-puh-nee) to go somewhere with someone

braille (BRAYL) a system of raised dots that are arranged to spell out words for blind people to read using their fingertips

breeds (BREEDZ) keeps animals so they can mate and produce young

canine (KAY-nine) a dog

climate (KLYE-mit) patterns of weather in a place over a long period of time

command (kuh-MAND) an order given to be obeyed

companion (kuhm-PAN-yuhn) an animal or person with whom one spends time

determined (di-TUR-mihnd) had a strong will to do something

disability (*diss*-uh-BIL-uh-tee) a condition of the body that makes it hard to do certain things, such as walk, see, or hear

disobey (*diss*-oh-BAY) to go against rules or commands

distracted (diss-TRAK-tid) having one's attention or concentration drawn away

donated (DOH-nay-tid) gave in order to help a charity or other group

estate (i-STAYT) a big house in the country on a large piece of land

guide dogs (GIDE DAWGZ) dogs that are trained to lead blind people from place to place

harness (HAR-niss) a device attached to an animal that allows people to hold on to the animal

headquarters (HED-kwor-turz) the main office of an organization

historic (hiss-TOR-ik) famous or important in history

independent (in-di-PEN-duhnt) free from needing the help of others

instructor (in-STRUHKT-ur) a teacher

military (MIL-uh-ter-ee) having to do with soldiers

pedestrians (puh-DESS-tree-uhnz) people who are walking

police dogs (puh-LEES DAWGZ) dogs trained to assist the police in activities such as finding missing people or sniffing out drugs

predict (pree-DIHKT) to say what one thinks will happen in the future

residents (REZ-uh-duhnts) people who live in a particular place

volunteers (*vol*-uhn-TIHRZ) people who work for no pay to help others

Bibliography

Ascarelli, Miriam. *Independent Vision: Dorothy Harrison Eustis and the Story of The Seeing Eye.* West Lafayette, IN: Purdue University Press (2010).

Frank, Morris, and Blake Clark. *First Lady of The Seeing Eye.* New York: Henry Holt (1957).

Swanbeck, Steve. *The Seeing Eye (Images of America).* Charleston, SC: Arcadia (2002).

Read More

Hall, Becky. *Morris and Buddy: The Story of the First Seeing Eye Dog.* Morton Grove, IL: Albert Whitman & Co. (2007).

McDaniel, Melissa. *Guide Dogs (Dog Heroes).* New York: Bearport (2005).

Patent, Dorothy Hinshaw. *The Right Dog for the Job: Ira's Path from Service Dog to Guide Dog.* New York: Walker & Co. (2004).

Learn More Online

Visit these Internet sites to learn more about Buddy and other guide dogs:

www.guidedog.org

www.guidedogs.com

www.seeingeye.org

www.tnhistoryforkids.org/people/morris_frank

Index

About the Author

Meish Goldish has written more than 200 books for children.
His books *Soldiers' Dogs* and *Surf Dog Miracles* were each a Children's
Choices Selection in 2014. He lives in Brooklyn, New York.